THIS JOURNAL BELONGS TO:

_____

_____

_____

BiG F*cking dreams

A JOURNAL FOR BUILDING YOUR BRIGHTEST DAMN FUTURE

D. A. SARAC

Published by Sourcebooks
P.O. Box 4410, Naperville, Illinois 60567-4410
(630) 961-3900
sourcebooks.com

Printed and bound in the United States of America.
JOS 10 9 8 7 6 5 4 3 2 1

WHEN WAS THE LAST TIME YOU HAD A BIG FUCKING DREAM?

Seriously. When was the last time you had an off-the-wall, pie-in-the-sky, reach-for-the-damn-stars kind of dream? Do you remember it? Can you picture it in your head right now?

So why is it still only a dream?

Enter: Manifestation. Manifestation isn't all charging crystals, rising signs, and psychic readings. It's a no-bullshit way to get the life you've always wanted. It's confronting obstacles, tackling challenges, and trusting that you have what it takes to get your shit done. It's for the dreamers, the doers, and everyone ready to take charge of their own damn futures. If that sounds like you, then break out the tool belt, draw up the schematics, and get ready to actually reach for the damn stars.

It's time to build those big fucking dreams!

WHAT THE fuck IS MANIFESTATION AND DO I NEED A goddamn crystal?

REDEFINING MANIFESTATION FOR THE BULLSHITTER, BELIEVER, AND EVERY BADASS IN BETWEEN.

When you hear the word *manifestation*, you may think of crystal balls, tarot cards, and those people who ask for your star sign before your first name. But what if we told you that trusting the universe doesn't mean diddly shit if you aren't actually trusting in yourself? That fortune-telling means fuck-all if you aren't actively building your own fortune? That manifestation is more about making things happen than wishing for all that could be?

Manifestation is about turning your dreams into reality—but it's not all meditating and putting out those ~good vibes~. It means putting in the work to create the life you've been yearning for. First, we're going to redefine manifestation. Then, we're going to teach you how to be grateful for the shit you have, attract the shit you want, and dream bigger than you ever possibly believed.

Let's unpack this shit. What comes to mind when you hear the word *manifestation*?

Why do you think people turn to manifestation, especially now?

OK, now for all those Negative Nellies out there, let's ditch the pessimism. Write down all the ways this could be bullshit.

All right, got that out of your system? Great, now cross off all that bullshittery and get back to work. There's nothing to lose in trying for the future you want!

I'M HAVING A

fucking Vision

ADD TO YOUR VISION BOARD TO START MANIFESTING YOUR FUTURE

What color aesthetic are you going for?

A. Soft, sweet colors. Put me in a fucking cloud.
B. Earthy cottagecore vibes because I'm basically a woodland sprite.
C. Bright, bold, primary colors—I want to be Oz up in this bitch.
D. Is black a color aesthetic?

What's one object you NEED on your board?

A. A private plane, train, and automobile—globetrotting here I come.
B. A stocked personal library with a sliding ladder, Belle-style.
C. All-access to my favorite foods and drinks. Did someone call for a fucking pizza party?
D. Just a Netflix subscription, please and thank you!

What dream companion are you adding?

A. Hello, fluffy animal sidekick!
B. Just me and my <3 soulmate <3
C. Haven't you heard of squad goals??
D. Um, I'd prefer a table for one, please.

mood swings

Now draw in objects for your own vision
board and fill this damn page!

What have been the biggest wins in your life? List five here.

What about those small wins? What are five things you conquered this fucking week?

OK, but what did you do to make those wins a reality? List all the steps you took to tackle those goals.

---

follow the
YELLOW BRICK ROAD...

OK, map out exactly what you've done to get this far on your path. Can you note the significant landmarks on your journey?

On a scale from 1 to 10, rate how prepared are you to

take on the future

LET'S
FUCKING GO

10

9

8

7

6

5

4

3

2

1

SCARED SHITLESS

Define what *hope* means to you. Why do you think it is so powerful?

What is one small thing you'd like to bring into your life this coming year? Write it here, and don't you forget it.

And what's one small action you can take today to get you one step closer to attaining that goal?

OOH they cute

The law of attraction is based on the belief that if you send out positive energy into the world, positive energy will then return. So, let's attract some good shit today! Write down five things you're hoping to attract and then five affirmations to match. Say those affirmations every damn day.

I'm naturally attractive	Affirmative
☐	☐
☐	☐
☐	☐
☐	☐
☐	☐

What do you want more of in your life? Fill the fucking page with those big wants.

_____

_____

_____

_____

_____

_____

_____

_____

_____

_____

_____

_____

_____

_____

_____

_____

What's a thing or quality that, if you had it in your arsenal, would feel too good to be fucking true?

_____

_____

_____

_____

_____

_____

What's stopping you from getting that thing or fostering that quality?

_____

_____

_____

_____

_____

_____

LET'S GET IT OMMM

It's meditation time! Get cozy, and set a timer for ten minutes. Meditate on what you want to manifest in your life. Think of it as if it's already happened. What emotions did you experience or note?

All right, now script out the future you saw. Use the first person as if it's already happened. Fill this fucking page!

DO IT FOR THE *vibe*

Check off all the words that describe the energy you're trying to have this coming year:

- Magical
- Empowering
- Radiant
- Soothing
- Compelling
- Exuberant
- Secure
- Impressive
- Mysterious

- Popular
- Creative
- Glorious
- Unstoppable
- Refined
- Quiet
- Warm
- Gracious
- Free

- Ambitious
- Fierce
- Content
- Authentic
- Harmonious
- Bold
- Captivating

OK, now write the one that speaks to you the most. Circle it big.

What are three things you can do in the next month to exude that energy?

✦

✦

✦

If the energy of your past year could be summed up by one word, what would it be?

Write down a time when something or someone stopped you from doing what you wanted.

Now describe what it would've looked like if you had ignored that stupid-ass barrier and did exactly what you wanted.

_____

_____

_____

_____

_____

_____

_____

_____

_____

_____

_____

_____

_____

_____

_____

moon
MADE ME DO IT

Create a new custom horoscope sign to describe you. Draw and name the symbol, then fill out the characteristics below.

Symbol: _____

Ruling element: _____

Strengths: _____

Weaknesses: _____

Likes: _____

Dislikes: _____

Compatible with: _____

Now write your horoscope for the day.
Take charge and go after it!

OK, now how does this sign tend to approach the future?*

**Number these items in order of importance, from
1 (a huge fucking must!) to 10 (not on my damn radar)**

- Taking a vacation this year

- Meeting up with family I haven't seen in a while

- Signing up for a new class

- Buying some loungewear (tie-dye optional)

- Ordering a book from an indie bookstore

- Posting five inspiring Instagram photos

- Uninstalling TikTok

- Lying on a hammock in the sun

- Calling a friend to catch up

- Creating an original sea shanty song

You think you're the queen of self-care yet?
Select True or False, then see how you do.

T F   If I manifest something, it'll drop right in my fucking
lap. Easy-peasy.

T F   I know there's a plan for me, and it's gonna be damn
good!

T F   All I need to do is think about what I want, and it will
happen.

T F   If I figure out what I want, I'll then be able to go after
it.

T F   The energy I put out into the world is what will return to
me.

T F   If I think about manifesting my goals every day, I'll
start to attract them.

T F   Manifestation is just fuckery, and my dreams are
unattainable.

If you said true to that last one, stop what you're doing and go
back to the beginning. We've got a whole lot of work to do!

ON THE *damn* bright side

DISCOVER THAT ATTITUDE OF GRATITUDE FOR EVERYTHING YOU ALREADY HAVE

Before you can build the future you want, you need to look around and get fucking grateful for all the things you already have! Gratitude is the true starting point—it gives us our foundation to build our sturdy-ass castle in the clouds.

Look around and take in all the things you have surrounding you. Take stock of the people who have already shaped your life. Bask in the lessons you've learned, the goals you've worked for, and all the goodness you've already created.

Gratitude helps us appreciate the big and the small. It urges us to live positively, relish good experiences, and bring forth so much more to be grateful for! It also gives us the opportunity to be grateful for all that has yet to come. So get ready to stand up and say "thank you very fucking much" for all the brilliance in our world.

Don your glasses of graciousness and take a peek at all those bright fucking spots shining in your life.

OK, brain dump time. Write all the things you are grateful for in this moment. There should be no white spaces on this page.

Now, what's one of your happiest memories?
Record the sunshine here.

Grab a blanket and head outside. Sit for five minutes and just soak in the moment. What are five things you are glad you're experiencing right fucking now?

_____

_____

_____

_____

_____

_____

_____

_____

_____

_____

_____

_____

_____

_____

SO TOTALLY
last season

Write a joyful habit that comes with the change of the seasons. That first open window in the spring? Pumpkin spiced coffee in the fall? Go ahead. Find the joy all over the fucking calendar.

Winter:

Spring:

Summer:

Fall:

ooh, THAT'S THE GOOD STUFF!

Check off all the things that are satisfying as hell.

- [ ] The smell of a freshly cut lawn, pastoral AF.

- [ ] Even vacuum lines in shag carpet, retro satisfying.

- [ ] You don't need artistic talent to watch those perfect calligraphy videos.

- [ ] Intensely designed dominoes falling all at once—ooh, hell yes!

- [ ] Popping. Motherfucking. Bubble. Wrap.

- [ ] That perfect eyeliner swoop.

- [ ] Peeling the plastic covering off of a new phone screen. *swoon*

- [ ] Landing in a new country and taking those first steps outside.

- [ ] I mean, have you ever found that one shirt that is the PERFECT soft material?

- [ ] The rush of ticking off an item on the to-do list.

- [ ] Bra off, motherfuckers.

- [ ] Hearing that song play during an outdoor concert that makes you feel invincible. Straight up magic.

- [ ] Click + Purchase = Endorphins.

- [ ] Standing outside under the sun with nothing to do and nowhere to be. *chef's kiss*

What's an opportunity that you were really happy you took?

_____

_____

_____

_____

_____

_____

What about a challenge that you had to overcome? What did
you learn from that experience?

_____

_____

_____

_____

_____

_____

_____

_____

What three everyday objects get you through the day?
Give them a shout-out here!

What is something in your home that just makes you deliriously
happy?

What's a quality you have that you want to thank today, because you know it's going to be instrumental in building your BFD (Big Fucking Dreams)?

PAGING RESIDENT *badass*

All right, class: anatomy time. For each body part below, label why you appreciate the hell out of it!

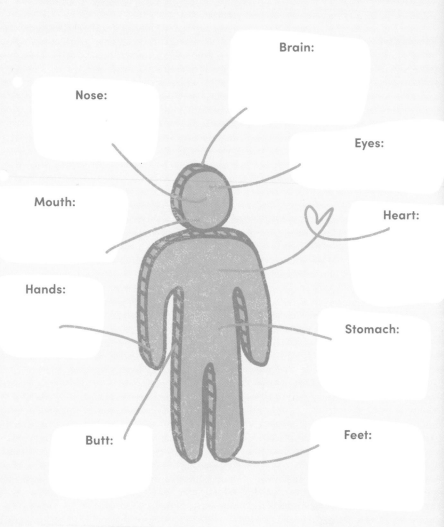

Brain:

Nose:

Eyes:

Mouth:

Heart:

Hands:

Stomach:

Butt:

Feet:

BACK ON MY *spy shit*

You have to head out on a secret mission and leave your old life completely behind. What three mementos are you taking with you? What does each one symbolize to you?

1. ....

....

....

2. ....

....

....

3. ....

....

....

How often do you thank a delivery, checkout, or postal person? If you didn't write anything down, get your ass out there and thank someone! Now come back here and get their response down.

oh happy
fucking day

Describe your happiest day possible. What makes it special as all hell?

_____

_____

_____

_____

_____

_____

_____

_____

_____

_____

_____

_____

_____

Let's say last year was a shitshow. Write down at least three things that were actually positive about it.

LEMONADE BREAK!

Pick a word for each of the following to give yourself a refresh of manifestation inspiration!

A. Noun _____

B. Adjective _____

C. Noun _____

D. Verb ending in -ing _____

E. Adjective _____

F. Noun _____

G. Something in your fridge _____

H. A liquid _____

I. Your favorite fucking curse word _____

Now fill in the blanks:

I've always wanted to be a _____

A

when I grew up, but my _____

B

_____ always got in the way. So tomorrow

C

I am _____ on my _____

D   E

_____, grabbing a _____

F   G

from the fridge, a bottle of _____, and

H

making that _____ shit happen.

I

When life gives you lemons, throw them at all the people who ever fucking doubted you

Write down why you're grateful for the following haters in your life, because they made you THAT much more extraordinary.

Your most recent ex:

Your high school bully:

Your work enemy:

That social media troll:

Did someone say frenemy:

That person who is just. Fucking. Wrong:

The one who annoys the hell out of you and you're not quite sure why:

Your biggest critic:

Your greatest nemesis:

I LIKE
coffee

(AND MAYBE THREE PEOPLE)

How are you able to help others? What kind of energy does that bring into your life?

What is something you take comfort in?

A FEW OF MY FAVORITE DAMN THINGS

Here's a blank page—go fucking crazy! Draw all of your favorite everythings in one spot!

Now shout a big damn THANK YOU
for all these incredible gifts.

What mental, physical, or emotional wellness practice are you particularly thankful for?

I SEE
badassery
IN YOUR FUTURE

What's something
you're excited to
have in your future?

What's something you're already grateful for that hasn't yet come to be?

Why do you think it's important to be thankful for all of these wonderful possibilities?

What does positivity mean to you?

Even when you're having a tough day (month, year), why is it important to be positive (and not the toxic bullshit kind, the real fucking kind!)?

CHECK YOU OUT

Circle which of these bestseller titles describe where you are in your life right now.

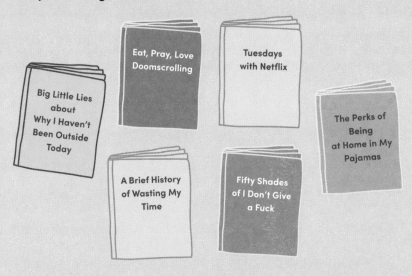

Eat, Pray, Love Doomscrolling

Tuesdays with Netflix

Big Little Lies about Why I Haven't Been Outside Today

The Perks of Being at Home in My Pajamas

A Brief History of Wasting My Time

Fifty Shades of I Don't Give a Fuck

Now circle the title that represents where you want to be a year from now (or write in your own).

The Lord of the Flings

No Fault in Our Star Signs

The Age of Independence

The Hitchhiker's Guide to Exploring Everything

Girl, Never Interrupted Anymore Because

Show Some Damn Respect

Who is one person in your life you are extra grateful for? Write them a letter here. Now, what's stopping you from picking up a card and sending it their way?

Who is a favorite book, movie, or TV character who is particularly inspiring? Write why you're grateful for them today.

A DAY OF FUCKING
gratitude

Write down one thing you're grateful for at each point of your day:

Now keep a gratitude list for every day this week. Write down one thing each day that makes you fucking smile!

SUN

MON

TUE

WED

THU

FRI

SAT

WALKING ON
damn
SUNSHINE

Circle which below statements apply to you:

I am grateful for
my fucking present.

I am appreciative of
my fucking past.

I am hopeful for
my fucking future.

Hint: every damn one of these better be circled, you reigning
king of gratitude!

LET'S START WRITING YOUR OWN SELF-LOVE STORY

To go after your dreams, you have to respect the hell out of all the star qualities you have! Let's talk self-love, friends! Self-love is empowering as fuck. It's about standing up and saying, "I don't have to prove to you that I'm amazing, I already know I am a brilliant, radiant, star-bound goddess." Self-love is celebrating all the things that make you special, encouraging all the positive self-talk, and realizing that showing yourself love is necessary to becoming the person you're striving to be.

So, throw a damn party for all the things that make you YOU! All those attributes that make you stand out from the crowd. That make your dreams fucking possible. That make your future better than you ever could possibly believe.

It's time to hit the top of the charts and show off every chapter of your self-love story!

Get a jar and some strips of paper. Write down at least ten reasons why you are so goddamn amazing and repeat them right fucking here. Read five out loud in the mirror right the fuck now.

1. _____

2. _____

3. _____

4. _____

5. _____

6. _____

7. _____

8. _____

9. _____

10. _____

Now keep the rest in the jar for later.

This is now your self-love arsenal.

FILL THAT FUCKER UP.

Why do you think self-love is so damn important? Describe how you feel when you practice real self-love.

FORTUNE FAVORS THE
bad witches

You've seen tarot cards, right? Now, draw three images for your own tarot deck that represent how you see yourself, how others see you, and who you truly are.

GET MYSTICAL UP IN THIS BITCH.

What is your favorite fucking trait of all time?

Trick question—it's all of them.

I PUT A *fucking* spell ON YOU

WE'RE COOKING UP A BATCH OF "IDEAL YOU" POTION.

Write in the ingredients that you believe make up the ideal version of you.
Fill that fucker to the brim with all those positive traits.

Now circle the ingredients you already embody.

Hint: every fucking ingredient should be circled here because—
abracadabra—you already are the most ideal version of YOU.

What's one quality you have that you wish others knew about?

So, what's stopping you from telling the whole damn galaxy?

swipe right

Looks like you're looking to fall in love...with yourself! Create a dating profile to show off all your exceptional qualities.

> *Draw your face!*

I'm great to hang out with on a quiet weekend because _____

_____

I take pride in _____

_____

The hallmark of a good self-love relationship is _____

_____

☐ Check here if you've found your soulmate...and yes, this box BETTER be checked.

Identify ten personality traits you love about yourself. Like really, truly L–O–V–E.

1. _____

2. _____

3. _____

4. _____

5. _____

6. _____

7. _____

8. _____

9. _____

10. _____

Of those ten things, which are you most proud of? Why?

_____

_____

_____

_____

_____

What stops you from practicing true self-love daily?

_____

_____

_____

_____

_____

_____

_____

_____

How can you kick those barriers in the ass?

_____

_____

_____

_____

_____

_____

CHECK MARKS THE SPOT

Check off each item you've completed in ONE day. Repeat until you have every damn one down.

- ○ I smiled at my own reflection and said, "Damn, I look good today."

- ○ I wore whatever the fuck I wanted.

- ○ I ate a good, satisfying-as-hell breakfast.

- ○ I took an extra five minutes indulging in my hot shower.

- ○ I went one hour without scrolling social media.

- ○ I didn't check my email ONCE after work hours.

- ○ I gave myself a genuine fucking compliment.

- ○ I had some much-deserved me-time.

You have so many fan-fucking-tastic qualities, but maybe there is an itty-bitty one you want to work on. What is it, and how will you nurture it to be better than ever?

NACHO TYPICAL LOVE LETTER

Write a love letter to that very special someone in your life...YOU.
bonus points for making it extra cheesy

Self-care is a great way to show yourself some extra love.
What are some of your favorite self-care techniques?

_____

_____

_____

_____

_____

_____

_____

_____

_____

_____

_____

_____

_____

_____

_____

_____

GO WITH THE DAMN FLOW

Follow the flowchart to see which self-care activity you should treat yourself to this week!

What is your plan to care for your mental health this year? There better be a long-ass paragraph here.

SO YOU AGREE, YOU THINK YOU'RE
REALLY FUCKING PRETTY?

What are five physical features you absolutely love about yourself?

1. _____

2. _____

3. _____

4. _____

5. _____

All right, now what about five things you're just really
fucking good at? C'mon, time to show off now.

1. _____

2. _____

3. _____

4. _____

5. _____

What qualities do you admire most in others? Fill this damn page!

SOMEONE HAS A
secret admirer

Now of that list, pick out the ones you don't believe you embody—write them here.

OK, good. Now cross off every line in that motherfucking list, because guess what:

YOU ARE ALREADY MORE THAN ENOUGH.

A LIMITED EDITION
haute mess

What is your biggest strength?

And what makes you feel most confident?

NOW YOU'RE SPEAKING
my language

What is your self-love language?

When you're home alone, how do you like to spend your time?

A. Writing in my journal all the things I accomplished that day.
B. Cooking myself my absolute favorite food.
C. Hmm...some surprise delivery ice cream never hurt anyone?
D. Hobby time with just me, myself, and I.
E. A long, soothing shower and a face mask sounds really fucking nice.

Let's say you've had the shittiest fucking day. How do you cheer yourself up?

A. Ever heard of a burn book? Sometimes you just have to let it all out.
B. I wash my sheets so I can burrow into that fresh laundry smell later.
C. Add. To. Fucking. Cart.
D. Retreat to the couch for some alone time.
E. Sweat it out, motherfuckers.

Hooray! You've suddenly come into a shit-ton of money! What do you do first?

A. I say "holy shit" and then tell everyone I know!

B. Ever heard of investing? You're welcome, future me.

C. Dream house? MINE.

D. Time for the solo trip of a lifetime!

E. Hair done, nails done, everything fucking did.

I feel loved when...

A. I give myself that mirror pep talk.

B. I finish that to-do list in service of my number one: me.

C. I treat myself to that new sweater I've been eyeing.

D. I carve out a concentrated amount of time to just do what I want.

E. I fuel my body and get moving.

Your self-love language is:

Mostly As—Words of Affirmation; a true star at giving yourself the motherfucking compliment!

Mostly Bs—Acts of Service; you've got your own back.

Mostly Cs—Receiving Gifts; TREAT YO' SELF.

Mostly Ds—Quality Time; bravo, you are your own damn best friend!

Mostly Es—Physical Touch; your body is your fucking temple.

weather report
LOOKS LIKE A 100% CHANCE OF FUCKING SUNSHINE!

In what situations do you really shine? Write the ideal scenario to get you as bright as can fucking be!

What do you want people to remember you for?

THAT WAS, LIKE, SO TOTALLY RANDOM!

What's the super random thing that you're really fucking good at? Put it out into the world!

_____

_____

_____

_____

_____

_____

_____

_____

_____

_____

_____

_____

_____

_____

bippity boppity boo

OK, princess-to-be, time to get
ready for the self-love ball!

Wave your magic wand and turn each negative sentence into a positive affirmation.

There's no way I can do this. _____

_____

Ugh, I look terrible today. _____

_____

My body is so not perfect. _____

_____

I'm just not good at anything. _____

_____

All those other people are so much better than me. _____

_____

Wow, I'm so stupid. _____

_____

I'm never going to get better at this. _____

_____

Who do I think I am? _____

_____

I'm not worth it. _____

_____

I don't have a future. _____

_____

THAT WAS SOME MOTHERFUCKING MAGIC!

HAVE WE TRIED

turning
it off

AND

back on

AGAIN?

REBOOT THE BAD SHIT WITH GROWTH MINDSET

Oof. Ever run into a mistake that you wished never happened? Of course you fucking have! Mistakes are part of what makes us human (and really good ones, too!). Sometimes, when we're building our goals and manifesting our futures, something doesn't go quite right. Sometimes the goal we have isn't one we reach, we make a mistake that takes us down a different path, or we realize that what we're after isn't actually what we want at all! Long story short, sometimes whatever forces that are at work in the damn universe stop us from getting exactly what we want...and that's fucking OK!

The challenges, the mess-ups, the failures, the mistakes, all that bad shit actually makes us prepared for the future we're destined to have. It gives us the creativity to grow through the nos and find new paths. It shows us how to have grit and resilience in the face of all that's shitty out there.

This is an opportunity to Ctrl+Alt+Delete the negative and power up the real future of your dreams.

What's one thing you did yesterday that you just want to Ctrl+Alt+Delete?

And what's one mistake or misstep you've made that still haunts you to this day? Write it here.

OK, got it. But think for a second. What's a lesson you learned from that shitty-ass thing?

YOU'VE GOT TO BE...

Oh dang, you've reached a fork in the road. Which option do you choose?

Time to sign up for those extracurriculars! Drama and basketball both catch your eye, but which do you choose?

A. Getcha head in the basketball game!

B. No one can stop me from getting that lead!

Welp, school was fun and all, but time to enter the real world. You have two job offers, one at a nonprofit for your passion project and the other at a very prestigious corporation. You choose...

A. Nonprofit! Passion over pennies!

B. The corporate job—higher salary means I can support my passions in other ways, duh.

...FORKING KIDDING ME

OK, you're ready for a change of scenery, but two places have caught your eye. One in the heart of the city, the other with that country charm. Which do you go for?

A. Bright lights, big city, baby!

B. Country all day, every day.

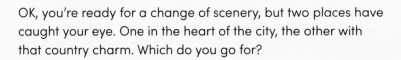

Cutie alert! You got a message from that old crush of yours. They're in town and want to grab dinner. You...

A. Respond "heck yes" and run to put on your favorite stunner outfit!

B. Respond "maybe next time." They aren't really your type anymore anyway.

Did you choose mostly As or Bs? It doesn't fucking matter, because each fork in the road led you down a new and exciting path. Repeat after us: **THERE ARE NO WRONG FUCKING CHOICES HERE.**

YET LEVEL
activated

Did you know that "yet" is a powerful fucking word? When we're looking at those big-ass challenges or those things we haven't quite mastered, give yourself the grace of a yet. Because, hell, we're all still learning here.

OLD ME	NEW ME
I don't know how to do this.	I don't know how to do this YET.
I made a mistake, and I'm not sure where to go from here.	I made a mistake, and I'm not sure where to go from here YET.
I haven't figured this out.	I haven't figured this out YET.

All right, you get the picture. Now rewrite your own negatives with the power of yet!

NEGATIVES	POSITIVES

You have the opportunity to shut down and restart your day.
What will you do that's different?

----

oopsie daisies

Describe a past mistake or decision that fucked you up at the time, but now you feel it was probably for the best.

CACTUS MAKES PERFECT

Stop being a prickly bitch and start letting your garden grow with growth mindset! Growth mindset means that instead of our character, intelligence, and creative ability being static, we can continuously learn and stretch ourselves to solve new problems. So, stop seeing failure as evidence that you succa a lot, but as an opportunity to grow beyond your wildest expectation!

Write down three challenges you've faced in the past.

Now, write down one thing you can explore to help you learn how to overcome that challenge next time!

What does growth mindset mean to you?

How can you use growth mindset to build toward the future you're striving for?

Describe a time where you put forth your best effort but you didn't quite meet your goal. What did you learn from that experience?

_____

_____

_____

_____

_____

_____

You *so* messed up at the meeting or party yesterday. Big time. Write a note to yourself that showcases a little grace for your mistake.

_____

_____

_____

_____

_____

JUST SAY *yikes* AND MOVE ON

It's Saturday night, and you've watched every damn show on Netflix, so now you're bored out of your mind. Come up with something new to do that you've never done before. What is it? How did it pull you out of your shitty-ass mood?

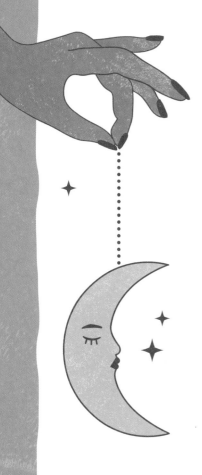

PIVOT! PIVOT!

All right, you've had your sights set on the following big fucking dreams, but something has gotten in your way. What do you do?

 You've been striving for that dream career, but you didn't land the job you wanted. You:

 That super cute Goldendoodle puppy has always been on your vision board, but your apartment doesn't allow pets. You:

 Your novel is really coming along, but suddenly the thought of getting it published is giving you the heebie-jeebies. You:

 Your dream house is finally on sale, but it's outside your price range. You:

A BLAST FROM THE PAST

Oh, look! You were able to Marty McFly this shit and go back in time! What is one thing you'd try to change?

How do you think that change would impact the future you're looking for?

All right, but what's stopping you from finding a new path toward that big-ass dream?

What does resilience mean to you?

When have you showcased some motherfucking resilience?

_____

_____

_____

_____

_____

_____

_____

_____

_____

_____

_____

Fill in the blank: When I was younger, I wish I would have:

ROLLS MY THIRD EYE

Sometimes our biggest mistakes come from not setting clear-ass boundaries. Sure, it's great to help others. But you also have to protect your own goddamn time. Rate these from 1 (I'll stop what I'm doing right this second!) to 10 (no fucking way—I've got my own shit to do).

A friend of a friend asks you to stop what you are doing and pick them up from Target. Oh, and this is the third time in one damn week.

Your brother or sister wants you to watch over your ailing parents for the day while they go on a shopping spree. Mind you, you're in the middle of a huge work presentation.

Your college kid needs to be picked up from a rowdy bar downtown. At night. Late. In the goddamn rain.

Your best friend calls right in the middle of a Zoom meeting after breaking up with their partner...for the fourth time.

You are swamped at your work-from-home job, but your dog is holding a toy just begging you to please go out and play.

The dreaded airport request. You are so fucking cozy in bed at some god-awful, no-one-should-be-getting-up time. But your sister is begging because she hates hailing taxis.

HANG YOUR WORRIES OUT TO FUCKING DRY

What are some of your biggest fucking worries about your future?

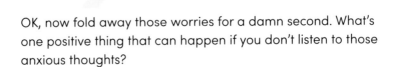

OK, now fold away those worries for a damn second. What's one positive thing that can happen if you don't listen to those anxious thoughts?

oh, the horror!

When you're about to make a big fucking decision, what are some of the things that little dude named Fear says to you?

Let's say you've been manifesting something for a while now but it just hasn't happened yet. How do you respond?

_____

_____

_____

_____

_____

_____

_____

Write down an action plan to finally help move the needle.

_____

_____

_____

_____

_____

_____

SHAME *SHAME* *SHAME*

Without looking it up, jot down the difference between embarrassment and shame. How do you handle each?

How do embarrassment and shame come into play when you're going after those big ol' dreams?

All right, now what can you say to cut out that negative bullshit? C'mon, write down your warrior cry here!

TIME FOR A FUCKING VACATION

You've done some great work here, and it's time for a damn vacation. What can you do if you take a vacation from your loudest negative thoughts? Write down three thoughts and then three things you can accomplish without them.

See you fucking never!

1.

2.

3.

Don't stay in touch!

1.

2.

3.

AH, THIS IS THE FUCKING LIFE, ISN'T IT?

PONYTAIL HIGH, GOALS FUCKING HIGHER

Oh, hello, high achievers, this is the part you've been waiting for, right? It's time to set those fucking goals! Goals help us conquer the world. They show us the benchmarks we want to hit, illustrate new behaviors we need to implement, and give us something to work for day in and day out. Goals help us focus on where we're going and let us visualize that big old life we have ahead.

Setting goals gives us the chance to think about what kind of life we truly want and motivates us to pursue it. If manifestation is setting our intentions for that dream future, goals are the building blocks to actually fucking get there.

So what's your end goal? What are you looking to achieve? And, more importantly, what are you going to do to get there? It's time to break up those big ideas into measurable, attainable goals.

Grab a scrunchie, whip that hair out of the way, and let's get to fucking work.

First up, why is it important to have clear fucking goals?

_____

_____

_____

_____

_____

_____

When you're thinking about your goals, what's the number one thing that gets in your way?

_____

_____

_____

_____

_____

OK, kick that fucker to the curb, we're not dealing with that shit anymore.

Make a list of ten things you want to get done this fucking month. Then rank them from most (1) to least (10) important.

1. _____

2. _____

3. _____

4. _____

5. _____

6. _____

7. _____

8. _____

9. _____

10. _____

* M A S H *

Time to take it back to grade school with a game of goal-setting MASH (Mansion, Apartment, Shack, House)! First fill in the options for the following categories. Make them as realistic or as off-the-fucking wall as you want! Then pick a number between 1 and 10. That is your magic number!

Now for the fun part. Count each of the category options until you reach the magic number. Cross out the option you land on. Repeat until you have a winner! Repeat for each category and then fill in your big-ass goals below!

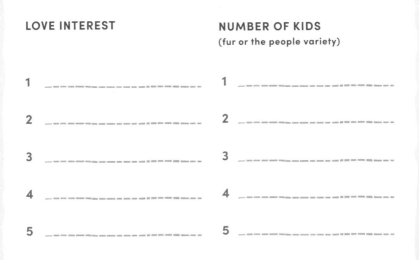

LOVE INTEREST

1 _____

2 _____

3 _____

4 _____

5 _____

NUMBER OF KIDS
(fur or the people variety)

1 _____

2 _____

3 _____

4 _____

5 _____

CAREER

1 _____

2 _____

3 _____

4 _____

5 _____

MODE OF TRANSPORTATION

1 _____

2 _____

3 _____

4 _____

5 _____

MONEY-MAKING HOBBY

1 _____

2 _____

3 _____

4 _____

5 _____

You live in a _____ with _____ .

You have ___ kids and are a high-achieving _____ .

You look fly as hell driving your _____ and in

your spare time make a little extra money by _____ .

goal digger

What was the last goal you set that you thought was too damn high?

So, what did you do about that unreachable goal? Did you get there?

Are you better at planning, delegating, or making that shit actually happen? Why?

YOU'RE DOING FUCKING GRATE!

Think about the biggest thing you want to tackle in the next year. Write ten bits of advice for yourself as you go after that goal.

1. _____

2. _____

3. _____

4. _____

5. _____

6. _____

7. _____

8. _____

9. _____

10. _____

All right, gouda job. Now, we know it might feel cheesy, but write a letter to yourself as if you've just achieved that goal. PRAISE BRIE!

COULD-A, SHOULD-A, WOULD-A

Make a list of all the possible events or reasons that could
maybe keep you from reaching that big plan of yours.

A sudden tornado

The internet goes down

Now repeat after us:
I DON'T CARE, I'M FUCKING DOING IT ANYWAY!

When you really fucking want something, how do you prepare the warrior in you to make it happen?

PANTS OR NO PANTS?

When writing a story, a plotter is someone who has a clear outline they follow. A pantser, on the other hand, tends to fly by the seat of their pants. When it comes to your goals, which are you?

Time to build your own wheel of fortunes. Fill out each category of the wheel with one goal you want to set for yourself in each category.

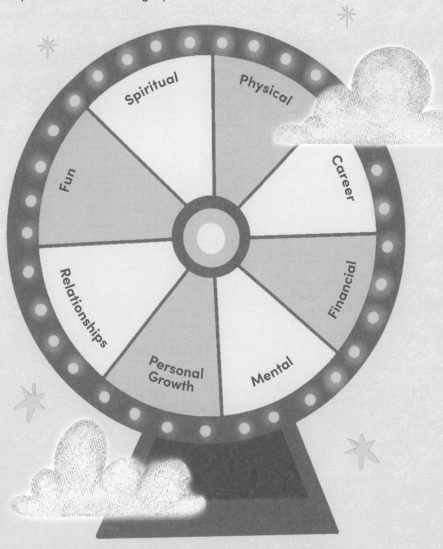

Now "spin" that fucking wheel and get started on one of your goals today!

LO MEIN, *high standards*

All right, you're getting pumped to tackle your to-do list, and so you order some celebratory takeout (you know, goal-getter fuel). Write out your three fortunes to get you motivated as fuck!

VOLUME UP, MOTIVATION HIGHER

Write down ten songs on your motivation playlist. Now crank up that volume and rock out all week long!

1. _____

2. _____

3. _____

4. _____

5. _____

6. _____

7. _____

8. _____

9. _____

10. _____

BLANKS ARE WORTH DOUBLE

Fill in the missing letters in our goal-setting word bank.

PR _ SP _ _ IT _

AC _ I _ VE _ _ NT

M _ NI _ _ ST

V _ SU _ _ IZ _

C _ _ EBRA _ _ ON

S _ _ CES _

V _ _ _ OR _

E _ _ O _ T

shit happens

What do you do if your plans get fucked up? Let's find out...

You've been working toward a big outdoor picnic with your family. Then a storm hits.

A. Give the food to your family members and then head back home.
B. Fuck it. I have too much work to do anyway.
C. Umm, INDOOR PICNIC!!!

You have a whole damn day to burn through your to-do list. Then your bestie calls because they're bored.

A. Press pause. I can reprioritize later.
B. Rip up the to-do list. I'm never getting to it anyway.
C. Sorry bestie, duties call.

You've carefully planned a staycation for some much-needed TLC. Then that shithead boss calls you to come in.

A. Cry a little, negotiate at least one day off, then head to the office.
B. Head straight in, because fuck it. I'll probably be fired otherwise.
C. Say sorry, but my PTO is in and I am fucking out!

Mostly Cs—Look at you, you goal-setting KING!
because your goals fucking matter.
Mostly Bs—Wooo buddy, please start this journal all the way over again
Mostly As—You're a little wishy-washy about whose goals come first.
Answers: If you picked...

action hero

OK, pick one goal you want to reach this fucking year. Write it here.

Now lay out a detailed action plan to make it happen. Set check-in dates. Build a timeline. Write out all those little steps.

Now don your cape and go make that goal happen.

When you accomplish something, does it have to be perfect, or are you OK with a "pretty darn good" or even an "at least you tried"?

How does the idea of perfection stop you from reaching for the things you want?

cover your tracks

Pick five habits you want to integrate into your life this month, then track them here by marking the square each time you do that habit.

What's one bigger habit you'd like to integrate for the rest of your life?

DOOOON'T STOP ACHIEEEVIN'

Here are some common qualities of high-fucking-achievers. Sort the words in the bank into one of the columns.

Action-oriented   Optimistic   Visionary   Clutter-free

Organized   Persistent   Flexible   Intelligent   Go-getter

Disciplined   Curious   Creative   Outgoing   Resilient

Passionate   Excitable   Wise

Oh yeah, that's totally me	Hmm...working on it...

smart AF

All right, now consider all of your damn goals and see if they're SMART (specific, measurable, achievable, realistic, timely). As a test, think of one goal and check all that apply.

- ☐ I know exactly what I want to accomplish—clear as fucking day.

- ☐ I see what I need to do to meet this goal, and you know I have a plan to do it.

- ☐ I've researched and am certain I can give the effort needed to meet my goal.

- ☐ I understand why this goal is worth accomplishing.

- ☐ I have a deadline ready and raring to go.

Now write a new SMART goal:

S (State what you'll do): _____

M (Provide a way to evaluate): _____

A (Describe how it's within your scope/achievable): _____

_____

R (Explain why it's important): _____

T (Give a specific timeframe): _____

Wow, look at you, A+ student! Class fucking dismissed!

WHY STOP AT QUEEN?

bitch, i am a

goddess

HAVE FUN WITH THOSE
BIG FUCKING DREAMS

Have you ever dreamed of ruling your own kingdom? Of being an astronaut? Of your paintings hanging in the Louvre? What if you lived in the Italian countryside and ate world-class pasta for every meal? Or if you landed on Jupiter, alien-style? When did we stop indulging in these big fucking dreams?

It's time to stop stifling our creativity and just let ourselves wonder about those high-reaching, pie-in-the-fucking-sky what-ifs! We don't want you to be queen of your kingdom, we want you to shoot for the stars and be the goddess of your own goddamn galaxy!

You know what your goals are, but what about those dreams? The massive ones! The ones you had as a kid and abandoned along the way. It's time to have some fun visualizing all the cool things you could ever possibly (or even impossibly) be! Be playful! Be bold! Be fucking confident in all the experiences that would be cool as fucking hell. And then, what if...what if you actually did just a few of them?

Bow down, because the motherfucking goddess has arrived.

IN A LAND FAR, FAR AWAY

Time to draw your own fantasy map. Name your continents, note the mountain ranges, rivers, magical forests, and add and name your cities. Build your motherfucking kingdom!

Now write your own fantasy story to go along with your kingdom. Who are you in that world? What are you after?

ANYTHING YOU CAN DO...

Pick your biggest idol. Now put yourself in their illustrious
shoes. Describe your life!

...I CAN DO FUCKING BETTER

Perfect. Now outline the qualities you think got you to that dream life.

_____

_____

_____

_____

_____

_____

_____

_____

_____

_____

_____

_____

_____

_____

_____

Damn it, your neighborhood is the only surviving region after a zombie attack. You're the leader, of course. What's your first move?

All right, now write the supply list for your most badass zombie bunker. What are you stockpiling?

OUT OF *fucking* OFFICE

Well, congratu-fucking-lations, you've won a month vacation!
Where are you going? Write out your dream itinerary here.

STAY WILD,
moon
CHILD

Sit in a quiet room, close your eyes, and imagine your dream reality. Now write down all the details here.

---

out of this world

It's time to get in that rocket ship and head out to a new colony on Mars. What five people will you assign to your crew? What roles will they have?

Mayday! Mars turned out to be a major drag. You're settling on your own planet now. Draw it here. What are you calling your new civilization?

witches GET RICHES

Holy shit, you've won ten million dollars and a whole year off to spend it all. Check off all the adventures you would choose.

- ☐ Fly all of your friends to a European castle for a month.

- ☐ Pay for a quick guest spot on your fave TV series.

- ☐ Lie on the sundeck of a yacht in the Caribbean for the summer.

- ☐ Bling out a dope RV and travel the country.

- ☐ Buy a winery in an Italian villa near the sea.

- ☐ Run your own ski resort in the Alps for the winter.

- ☐ Hunker down in a woodsy remote cabin.

- ☐ Hit up every major fashion week to build the wardrobe of your dreams.

- ☐ Acquire a giant tract of land and open an animal rescue.

- ☐ Fill up that five-car garage.

- ☐ Design and build your dream home.

- ☐ Follow your favorite band on their global tour.

- ☐ Build up that priceless art collection.

- ☐ Deck out a four-room library with all the books you could imagine.

- ☐ Go on an adventure tour around the world.

- ☐ Start your own dream business.

You're really, really damn famous for something.
What is your skill?

Step into that time machine and turn a few dials.
Where in the past or future are you visiting? Why?

READ IT AND *weep*

Oh, hey, look at you, you published a book! What's the title and genre?

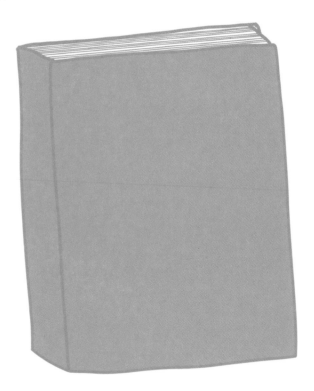

Great, now write a book review from your biggest fan!

★ ★ ★ ★ ★

_____

_____

_____

dreams DO COME TRUE

Think back to when you were a kid. What did you want to be when you grew up?

And now put on those kid glasses again. What would child you say about current you's big old dreams?

What's the best part of being you? The one thing that makes you high-five yourself?

You have a full week of dream meals to plan out. What're you eating for breakfast, lunch, and dinner?

OK, now visualize your perfect day—one whole day to do whatever you fucking want. What's it look like?

Now pick one part of that and just do it today. How did that feel?

evil genius VIBES

You're a brilliant inventor working on your next project. What is it?

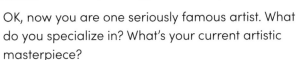

OK, now you are one seriously famous artist. What do you specialize in? What's your current artistic masterpiece?

REALITY CHECK

Over the next ten years, do you see yourself doing any of the following? Mark either **A (no fucking way), B (eh, maybe), or C (fuck yes)** next to each.

_____ Drastically change careers.

_____ Extreme makeover, me edition (hair, clothes, attitude).

_____ New city, here I come!

_____ Become a list-master and organize the shit out of everything.

_____ Oh hell yes, dream vacation.

_____ Gonna put myself out there and join that club.

_____ Adopt a new pet.

_____ Volunteer for my dream organization.

_____ Change my name.

_____ Challenge myself with a new hobby.

Results: if you have at least one fuck yes, then you're winning.

Time to take a big-ass risk. What daredevil thing are you signing up for?

Dream career time! If money didn't matter, what dream career would you build for yourself?

Draw a picture of your perfect home here. What does it look like? Who are you sharing it with?

All right, you're a badass ghost now. Who are you haunting?

And now you can be any supernatural creature you want. Which do you choose?

I'M INTO COLD PIZZA AND
spiritual shit

Check off the experiences you'd be into trying.

☐ Go parasailing.

☐ Take the train from one side of the country to the other.

☐ Design a popular clothing item.

☐ Discover a hidden artifact on a remote island.

☐ Work your way up to a black belt in martial arts.

☐ Teach classes in the subject of your choice.

☐ Get a degree in something you love.

☐ Play an instrument in an orchestra.

☐ Sing in a band.

☐ Paint a mural.

☐ Travel to a far-off location.

☐ Sleep under the stars.

CROWNS
ARE ALWAYS IN FASHION

Time to pick your perfect power outfits to conquer the future of your dreams.

You're making a big fucking decision today and want to exude confidence. You throw on:

A. Your favorite power suit. Classic badass.

B. Your most regal gown—remind them who the fuck you are.

C. One word for you: Leather. Intimidating AF.

Your enemy is coming along to challenge your power. What are you keeping by your side?

A. Your inner circle is the best accessory.

B. Jewels fit for a fucking queen.

C. I think a sword will do?

All right, but now you need to charm your way through the day. What do you put on?

A. Going casual—joggers and a tee will put everyone at ease.

B. Some pastels will make me a total softy (little do they know).

C. Just a smirk.

OK, now you need your most magical accessory. You grab:

A. Your crystal ball—you make the best decisions when you know what future is in store.

B. Who needs a wand when you have a fucking magic scepter?

C. An unconquerable shield. Everyone stand back.

What's the biggest dream you've ever had?

_____

_____

_____

_____

_____

_____

How does it feel imagining all these possibilities?
How does it stretch the boundaries of what could be
possible?

_____

_____

_____

_____

_____

DAILY REMINDER:

I AM A

fucking

goddess

IT'S A
beautiful day
TO
get shit done

DON'T STOP UNTIL YOU'RE FUCKING PROUD.

Congratulations, you badass—you know where you've been and you know where you want to go. Now let's take some fucking action. It's important to reach for the stars and manifest your dreams, but it's even more important to start building the rocket to get there.

So get off your ass and get to damn work! What can you be doing today, tomorrow, and all the days after to achieve all the things on your list? How can you zero in on what you truly want to accomplish? Having dreams is empowering as fuck, but making the moves to get there? Well, that's straight king shit.

It's time to unleash yourself on the world and start knocking out those goals one by one. Because you, my friend, are a force to be fucking reckoned with.

Gut check time. How far do you feel from living your dream life?

If your dream feels too far away, what are the things you most want to change?

OK, now list one thing you can do to make that fucking change today.

ONE STEP AT A FUCKING TIME

Let's get this goal thing going. Think of what you want to get done this year. Check off each item as you finish.

GOAL:

- [ ] Wrote the start date on my calendar in gi-fucking-normous letters.

- [ ] Set a concrete timeline (remember those SMART goals?).

- [ ] Wrote the name and number of a friend to hold me accountable.

- [ ] Told the people around me so the news was out.

- [ ] Made a list of any materials I might need along the way.

- [ ] Identified the first step needed to get this big-ass dream going.

- [ ] _____

- [ ] _____

Sometimes moving forward requires us to leave something behind. What habit do you have that probably should fucking end already?

_____

_____

ON THAT visionary shit

OK, what does your
end-of-year vision look like?

What about your five-year plan?

So what does your ten-year plan look like? And be as fucking specific as possible.

HELLO
sunshine

Create a productive and stress-free morning routine for yourself. Write it here.

THE BAGS UNDER MY EYES ARE
designer

Holy hell, getting up in the morning is not always easy. Come up with one technique that'll help you conquer those not-so-motivated days.

COMFY, COZY, AND ALL THAT SHIT

All right, draw your comfort zone.

Now write all the things outside of it that you want to try. Push yourself to pick one of these today. Soar beyond that motherfucker.

Sometimes we veer off course—what's one motivating intention to get you back on the path toward your dreams?

Write it here BIG AS FUCK.

Jingle ALL THE WAY

Design a campaign slogan to highlight what your next year has in store. Bonus points if it rhymes.

Describe your happy place. When things get hard, turn back to this page and visualize yourself here.

Audacious
as fuck

What are your top three priorities in the coming year?

1. _____

2. _____

3. _____

I SEE YOUR FUTURE, AND IT IS

fucking

bright

It's ten years from now and you've accomplished what you've set out to do. Write a letter to the person you are right now thanking them for all the hard work they put in. Make it fucking lit.

When you think of your past, how do you feel?

LEGWARMERS: ON
CORE WORKOUT: ACTIVATED

It's time to talk about our core values. Our personal values should guide every goal and decision we make for ourselves. They're our internal gut check—our guideposts as we move through life. Check the five values that you want to focus on while you build your future.

- Wealth
- Security
- Reputation
- Openness
- Meaningful Work
- Service
- Respect
- Love
- Leadership
- Justice

- Happiness
- Learning
- Loyalty
- Family
- Influence
- Peace
- Growth
- Fun
- Curiosity
- Creativity

- Humor
- Beauty
- Authority
- Autonomy
- Compassion
- Achievement
- Friendship

How have your core values changed over time?

How do you expect them to evolve in the future?

FILL THE *fuck it* BUCKET

Time for a bucket list! List ten things you 100% must accomplish in the next ten years.

1.
2.
3.
4.
5.
6.
7.
8.
9.
10.

Now, if you could only choose one of them to go after, which one would it be?

Great, now you've solidified your number one damn priority.

ALL RIGHT, EXAM TIME.

Circle whether each statement is True or False.

T F Planning just makes your dreams boring.

T F What you wear/how you look dictates the dreams you can attain.

T F You shouldn't ask for help to reach your goal.

T F If your dream doesn't come true quickly, then forget about it.

T F Only start short-term goals.

T F Visualizing your goal does absolutely nothing for results.

T F Only plan one goal or dream at a time.

T F Only start new goals. Last year's will never go anywhere.

T F Sometimes a dream is just too big to really happen.

T F Sometimes a barrier is a sign to change your dream.

Answers: if there's one fucking True circled here, start this journal all the fuck over again.

What boundaries do you need to put in place to get your goals going?

_____

_____

_____

_____

_____

_____

_____

_____

_____

_____

_____

_____

_____

_____

_____

Ha ha ha, no.

You can only handle so much in a day, for fuck's sake. Let's practice setting those boundaries and saying a big old "no!" Practice each one of these in the mirror, then circle your go-to boundary-setting response.

Whisper a sweet "no <3" with a wink.

Dramatic pause.......... "no."

Give a sassy over-the-shoulder "no" as you walk away.

A long, drawn-out "nooo" with a built in ? at the end.

Scowl with an emphatic "no."

Classic side-eye "nah."

Raised eyebrows, hands on hips, and a head-shaking "no fucking way."

Firm "no" with a controlled smile.

What does productivity mean to you?

_____

_____

_____

_____

_____

_____

Describe a time when you were really fucking productive.
What was driving you forward?

_____

_____

_____

_____

_____

_____

How can you harness that energy for your upcoming dreams?

What do you need to get your shit organized? Go get it today.

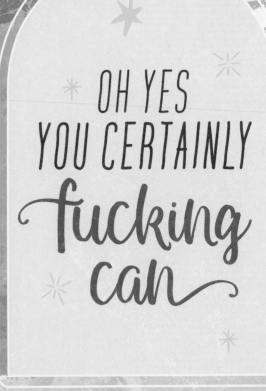

OH YES
YOU CERTAINLY
fucking
can

WE'VE GOT SPIRIT, YES WE DO!

Write a motivational cheer that will get you through the really fucking hard days.

**Write it on a Post-it and stick it to your mirror.
Remember it every damn day.**

Now who's in your cheerleading squad? List your support system here. Don't you dare try to go this thing alone!

STAR? LOL NO. I'M A DAMN
constellation

Think again to the biggest goals you want to achieve. Harness that star power and come up with an affirmation to help you conquer each and every fucking one.

Which figures or mentors inspire you? Link specific goals with specific mentors who can help you through.

How do you define passion? Are you ready to lead your most passionate life?

After all this work, how do you feel about the future now?

We're coming full circle here. How do you now view manifestation? Your first and last answers in this journal better not fucking match.

CONGRATULATIONS, YOU ARE MAGICAL AS FUCK.

TAKE CHARGE OF THOSE

BIG
F*CKING
dREAMS

LOG YOUR BIG FUCKING DREAMS

Fill this ongoing list with all those dreams—big and small. Then conquer the whole damn world.

___/___/___

___/___/___

___/___/___

___/___/___

___/___/___

___/___/___

___/___/___

___/___/___

___/___/___

_ / / _

_ / / _

_ / / _

_ / / _

_ / / _

_ / / _

_ / / _

_ / / _

_ / / _

_ / / _

_ / / _

_ / / _

_/_/_

_/_/_

_/_/_

_/_/_

_/_/_

_/_/_

_/_/_

_/_/_

_/_/_

_/_/_

_/_/_

_____ / / _____

_____ / / _____

_____ / / _____

_____ / / _____

_____ / / _____

_____ / / _____

_____ / / _____

_____ / / _____

_____ / / _____

_____ / / _____

_____ / / _____

_____ / / _____

_/_/_

_/_/_

_/_/_

_/_/_

_/_/_

_/_/_

_/_/_

_/_/_

_/_/_

_/_/_

_/_/_

_/_/_

ABOUT THE AUTHOR

D. A. Sarac is a fiction editor, author, and playwright. Works include *Dream Big, Princess*; *The Newest Avenger*; *(Your Child) Saves the Day*; and *My Monster Friends and Me*, available from PutMeInTheStory.com and Sourcebooks. Her all-time favorite gig is being a mom to a beautiful, witty, and talented daughter. You can find her wearing a Radiant hat and alphabetizing newly learned curse words at **TheEditingPen.com**.

F*ck.